VR UX

2nd Edition

Dedicated to all current/former students that are buried in student loan debt because they tried to be educated ☺. Every cent earned from this book will go towards my own student loan debt.

You've been warned.

Do NOT take this work as "Commandment"- The world of VR UX is in its infancy and I wrote this to give the community a consolidated starting point. As the technology evolves and users express their tastes, the rules will change & best practices will morph. Start here and hopefully we will all end up in a better place than where we started.

I wrote this book to move fast for the new human trend of short attention spans, so I'll try to avoid the transitional *fluff* that sometimes extends non-fiction guides.

I owe a LOT of the credit to Oculus.com, Google, various VR bloggers (you know who you are), & The Voices of VR Podcast. Thank you for all your hard work in making virtual… a reality.

WHAT'S DIFFERENT IN VR UX?

Infants

When a human straps on a VR headset and begins a new experience it's as if they are an infant human immediately wondrous about their surroundings. The human will have some assumptions about the world based on the real-world mimicry found there but will not simply assume that everything behaves as it does in reality. They will explore and attempt to manipulate objects and movements to familiarize themselves with the rules of the new world.

While video games presented a similar experience once their worlds were deemed "realistic," the medium was stuck on a flat 2D screen and made exploration less primal. In VR, the player has to comprehend an entirely new dimension and will take longer than usual to familiarize themselves with the digital plane. Because of this, it's important to understand it's not as simple as porting 2D rules like "fitts law" into VR interaction design.

Most designers reading this book are used to designing for interfaces that afford inhuman interactions like scrolling and clicking. Instead of explaining inhuman interactions, you must prepare to inform the player of the human tendencies they can leverage and perhaps expose them to new ones they didn't know were there. Your users are infants and it's up to you to give them enough guidance to feel comfortable in your new world.

Metaphors become literal.

When designing for the web on desktop and mobile, we had to come up with new metaphors for user actions like scroll, click, tap, etc. Metaphors for VR will be more literal, scrolling = strolling, click = pick/point/grab, above the fold = before the horizon.

Perspective is Important

Inside of a VR headset, the player's perspective becomes their state of mind with a view similar to that of the real world. They are not on the outside looking in – but rather on the inside looking. Instead of creating a new language of standards like video games and computers did, VR should start with reality and chip away as the technology constrains.

As a designer, it's important to ground yourself because there are technological limitations that won't allow you to design for "real life." Unlike its predecessors, the VR screen experience dangles off the edge of reality. Players have spent their entire lives perceiving 3D space in the real world and will have some reality-based expectations. Designers have to strike a healthy balance on what should/shouldn't mimic our 3D reality with technical constraints in play.

Content rules for the experience have changed.

In VR, a user can control the display by simply moving their head. This changes the rules of how content is displayed. Right now, when you look at a computer/phone screen, your head movements are not tracked and don't invoke the content to change in an way. Instead, content changes are prompted by input devices and in the most similar scenario, the movement of the device itself. Now that a user can move their head in an environment in which you will have their full attention, it's important that the content responds to those movements in a pleasing & somewhat organic manner.

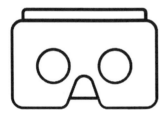

There are new affordances.

Affordances are the cues within an experience that become second-nature and are designed to be self-explanatory in terms of their use. The movement of a bent page corner indicating a page swipe on a mobile reading experience is one digital example of this. VR will produce its own set of affordances as designers get more feedback and the medium matures. These affordances can transfigure over time.

The first obvious affordances that will exist in VR will be the same affordances we have in the real-world absent of digital devices. Designing a door handle to be "pulled" instead of pushed or following a path of painted lanes on a road. Those affordances will naturally adapt from the ones we already experience. There will also be new affordances designed for immersive inputs. Already we see examples in VR content and the depth at which it's displayed to imply the order of importance. Picture Netflix recommending movies to you in VR where the most relevant are nearest to you and the second most relevant is the next nearest and so on.

The future of affordances in VR will be based in neuroscience. Subtle changes will be made to experiences based on what we learn from the science and each individual user as more devices require user input and track personal use.

Web & mobile designers have to grow into environmental designers.

The promise of VR is to be the next digital computing platform used by the masses for media, productivity & more. It's only fitting that digital designers build upon skills accumulated from work on prior platforms and adapt them for VR without forcing old standards. With mobile, web designers adapted their skills by considering the "where" – with VR it's going to be less about "where" the user is putting on the headset and more about the "environment" once they're wearing it. Inherently, there are more choices in an immersive environment than a computer/phone screen could ever offer. Because human curiosity is organically at play inside a VR experience, you have to focus more on the environment than in the past and account for multiple points of possible interest and response. The environment is the user interface and visa-versa. Environment designers have to be comfortable working with fewer constraints and more space that blurs that lines between what's UI vs. not.

More addressable screen space.

The environment experience brings more addressable screen space. Computers and phones came with constraints as designers had to work within fixed frames and edges. As a VR designer, you will crack the fixed edges and work with three-dimensional depth and layering. Fewer constraints is intriguing but comes with the manifestation of more error space.

Account for the player setup.

Players in our digital worlds are typically sitting comfortably in their stationary chairs while interacting with the screen and inputs. VR brings a few new conditions where a player may be asked to stand, move around, sit on a movable chair, or lay down. In your UX approach, you'll have to consider the player's setup – something most digital UX designers are not used to calling out.

More sketching than wiring.

Wireframing has long been Queen of the UX Designer planning toolbox for the computer/phone. Often, UXers will sketch out their embryonic ideas with characters, boxes and arrows but their final output to the developer ends up being a digital file. I'm not saying that VR UXers won't eventually find software that makes sense for VR storyboards, but as it stands, sketching is probably the most efficient way to get from concept to prototype. With VR, you have to build an environment on a rounded surface that isn't as simplistic as boxes and arrows and sometimes 3D sketch tools can slow you down in the details. This is evolving as Google Blocks and Sketchfab + Gravity are just some of the interesting programs providing sketch-like options for the inceptive phases of VR development.

Design Ideas Happen OFF the computer!

Up for argument but the "cool" promise of VR design is that you can run into a variety of "aha!" ideas as you navigate the real world and therefore this affords you to spend more time navigating reality than a computer screen to uncover new designs.

More freedom means more cues.

The user has more freedom in VR which means that cues are back! I know what you're thinking, cues failed on the web and computers. "I hated that Microsoft paperclip!" Traditionally, cues have been annoying on computers but have been key when it comes to video game storytelling. Also, the web is finally starting to experience cues that are less intrusive and more helpful. With time, companies figured out how to beautify them as parts of their sign up processes, forms, and how-tos.

Since users have more freedom to look away, you'll have to use cues in the form of sound, lighting, coloring, movement, character motion, and more to procure a sense of story control. Cues will ultimately direct the user down the experience path you want them to venture instead of getting lost in other details.

VR objects are not passive.

The objects placed around a VR world are not passive. They are autonomous which means they should respond to the changes in the world around them including other objects, settings and characters. Video game designers are used to accounting for this when they design worlds but most web/mobile designers are not. You'll have to get used to understanding the holistic impact of each object and the part they may play in the whole. Forget about designing objects in isolation.

Dream in spheres & skyboxes.

You'll have to throw away those flat design tutorials for a bit and retrain your mind to think in spheres. If you haven't worked in video game design, spend some time understanding skyboxes and skylines as they are critical for the end product. They can ground your user, set the mood, make the rest of the world more believable, and more. They are critical when designing VR worlds so you can forget the typical "I want a white background" statements from web design projects. To learn more, there's a great article online by product designer Tessa Chung titled, *Making Sense of Skyboxes in VR Design*.

The tech is fragmented. But it's different this time.

It may seem like web designer are used to fragmented tech because they have to account for desktop, mobile and then within those, different browsers and operating systems. The same software issues exist in VR development so you will wave a familiar hello to each but VR has a unique ecosystem in that the consumer tech is quite fragmented by quality. Yes, one could argue that there are low-end phones and high-end phones but most designers have exclusively worked on high-end smartphones and desktops.

Today, you'll find the majority of users playing with low-end VR devices but the most immersive experiences are found on lesser-used high-end setups. What gives? It's because low-end leverages a device that's already gone mainstream – the smartphone. High-end devices are somewhat complicated to setup and operate, not to mention costly. So the most important question you can ask yourself when initially dreaming up a VR idea is who am I trying to reach and why? That will ultimately guide you in whether or not you want to build a low end or high end experience first. Of course, you can do both but functionality dramatically differs (mostly the degrees of freedom) so most designers end up picking one.

Presence is EVERYTHING

The ultimate sin of a VR designer would be to explicitly break a user's sense of presence in the world you've created. The moment you remind them they are in a VR headset and they pay attention to any externalities of the real world or disbelieve the present virtual world, you have broken your design. The most important role you have as a VR designer is to bring the user in, alter their state of mind to be present in your world, and get your point across as they forget about the room they currently occupy. Do not remind them at any point that your world isn't their reality!

So is Multi-tasking a thing?

Not yet. As virtual evolves and blends into the world of mixed reality, perhaps. It's possible the next-gen of VR software updates support incoming phone calls, texts, and more but until then, we are fully immersing a user and assuming their other devices and goods are absent from the virtual biodome. (if you didn't get the *Biodome* reference it means you haven't seen the movie, and I feel bad for you).

UX STRATEGY IN VR

The VR UX Strategy Outline

1. Write a Short Narrative
2. Form Persona & Motives
3. Research & Pick Your Tools
4. Choose an Interaction Model
5. Sketch & Storyboard
6. Apply Sound, Cues, Inputs & Add-Ons
7. Develop Your Test Plan
8. Prototype & Adjust the Strategy

1. Write a Short Narrative

Take the time to write at least a paragraph describing the wanderlust virtual *storyworld* in your head. This is the best part of the VR UX process because it allows you to flex your creative freedom & wonder about a new platform with what seems to be limitless possibilities. So create – write a paragraph or more summarizing the story, environment, & experience that owns your imagination. You can jot down plot, characters, problems, scenery, objects, lighting, philosophy, etc. where it makes sense. Let your mind wander and build a dream narrative. Now get ready to bring it back to reality ☺ - virtual reality.

The narrative should give your team a reference of the "dream" state, which comes in handy when you hit walls. It's meant to provide a holistic decision map and sustain interest throughout the building process.

2. Form Persona and Motives

A VR UX strategy starts much like that of any UX strategy. You have to define the audience, depict that audience for the designers & developers. Then have the team agree on motives of the VR experience and the motives of the user.

I would assume that most of the UXers reading this book have near-puked over written material on how to form a persona so I won't spend a lot of time on it but here are some things to understand before you dive in

- Even if you think personas are useless, they matter quite a bit in VR right now because the technology is fragmented and new – so even if you don't believe in personas you should make the basic one, outlined here, before you dive in and develop
- You may want to create multiple personas for the same audience because the experience could vary from person-to-person
- VR isn't at the point yet where businesses are building VR sites like they do websites. So don't approach a VR UX persona with the intention that there's this HUGE internet audience that's going to use it

Person	Behaviors/Wants
Access	**Reactions**

- Person – Who?
- Behaviors/Wants – why would this fit into their life?
- Access - define how they will discover & access the tech – for instance, you wouldn't develop for Oculus if you were targeting grandmas for your experience – a smartphone would make more sense as they probably have one of those before they would have an Oculus
- What do you expect them to get out of the experience?

3. Research & Pick Your Tools

One of the primary steps in Persona development asks you to address "accessibility" and that's quite important right now because a small population of users has access to VR technology and an even smaller population owns VR headsets. We hope that VR will see the same mainstream adoption of other computing platforms like computers and phones but for now, reach is limited. Tool selection will be driven by your persona.

Put a bit of research into your audience's use of technology and find the point of interaction that can exist for them using "said" technology.

If your audience is highly technical or in-touch with gaming culture than you are probably safe designing for the Rift or Vive headset. Perhaps an urban profile would allow you to reach the same conclusions in that cities have access to high-speed internet and plenty of trendy vendors and touch points where one can interact with VR tech. If you are designing for the mom of a rural family, you would maybe want to consider developing for Google Cardboard since she is more likely to have a smartphone and the income to build or buy a simple cardboard headset. Let's address the different tiers of VR devices that exist in the market today:

High-tier devices

HTC Vive, Oculus, & Playstation VR are the primary high-quality VR headsets in 2017. These headsets are developed for the sole purpose of VR and require the tethering to a high-powered computer tower. They support 6 degrees of freedom (X,Y,Z depth) and allow for roomscale VR experiences. Each comes with 2 remotes, one for each hand. Users interact with experiences via the Oculus Store, independently hosted internet download, or Steam (a very popular computer game store)

- The advantage = gives users the most realistic experience possible increasing the likelihood of full immersion
- The disadvantage = volume of user is lowest among the tiers and access is limited due to the cost and difficulty to setup

Mid-tier devices

Google Daydream and Samsung Gear are the primary mid-tier headsets. They are made specifically for VR but require the use of a compatible smartphone. The tier has seen speedy growth compared to high-tier headsets. Both come with a single remote and include some control inputs on the device itself. Users interact with experiences via a mobile app or web.

- The advantage = a larger audience than high-tier headsets and more technical capabilities than the low-tier headsets – sort of the middle ground for VR developers today
- The disadvantage = audience is still somewhat limited and since it's using a mobile phone you have to make significantly more design sacrifices than you would developing for a high-tend headset. It only allows for 3 degrees of freedom (X,Y).

Floor-tier devices

Google Cardboard is the stand alone here. It's a simple cardboard case that you can strap most smartphones in and users interact with VR via a mobile app or web. It has already shipped over 5 million units and that's not even counting all the knockoffs and homemade cardboard headsets so it's mass appeal is .. well, appealing. So far, it's been a hit-or-miss experience for users. Video seems to be taking more precedence for this headset which makes sense since Google has YouTube skin in the game

- The advantage = the largest audience and has less hurdles to overcome with word-of-mouth support
- The disadvantage = Limits immersion because there are many sacrifices the VR designer has to make for low-end tech. It also only allows for 3 degrees of freedom (X,Y).

Pick your design tech.

There are a variety of options when it comes to designing your VR experience. I would imagine folks that call themselves "VR Designers" will spend most of their time on "digital" instead of video but I'll cover both for the HECK of it: Check out the design hierarchy below. You start at the top on the left or right side and work your way down.

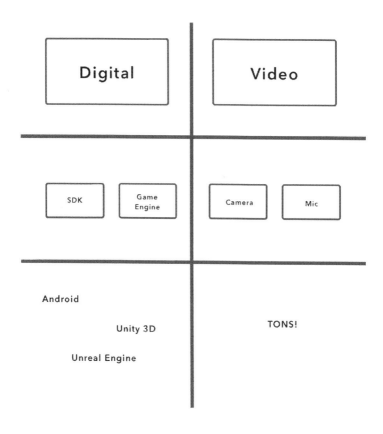

Digital VR design tech.

A VR designer can use native SDK's from the company behind your device-of-choice and/or use a game engine like Unreal Engine or Unity 3D to produce VR experiences. The latter is more popular because it strips away a lot of the technical underpinnings of creating a 3D world which require skills that most designers and even developers don't have. It's important to note that for this book we are focusing on VR headsets but there is an entire community focusing on how to make the desktop and mobile web virtual using WebGl, HTML5, Javascript and other languages that can build immersive experiences.

- Unity 3D and Unreal are both legitimate game engines that the VR community is leveraging. Which one you pick relies more on a pros cons list of the two that you can develop while browsing pro/con lists online – primary difference in structure is that Unreal is open-sourced while Unity is not. It's also been said that the learning curve for Unity is less steep but Unreal grants you advanced graphical performance
- Like any production work, a lot of what you design will have to compromise with the technical rendering requirements. Keep this in mind when thinking about elaborate worlds with thousands of interactions and design features

Once you have selected your tools, you can start to assign roles to members of your team and think through what's possible given your narrative. While you probably have a good idea of the tech you are planning to develop for now, I highly recommend you do your research on the costs, skills, limitations & access to all the tech mentioned here before you reach a final conclusion.

Video VR design tech.

Video is not nearly as far along as digital VR because 3D game development has existed for decades and 3D camera technology is embryonic.

There is no front-runner when it comes to the cameras being used to shot 360 degree video. Unfortunately, most of the best cameras are financially out of reach for the general designer (more on that in a hot minute).

There is no standard post-production software yet in the VR video space but each camera & rig companies promote the use of their own. Google is working on a "stitching" technology they claimed would be available for the public to use in 2016 but that google-owned tech has yet to see the light. Other than that, Kolor, which was acquired by GoPro, has been utilized by a lot of hobbyists that rely on a GoPro VR camera rig.

High-tier cameras

Lytro Immerge, Jaunt Neo, Nokia OZO, and Facebook Surround 360 are the most notable high-tier cameras for 360 degree video.

They have the ability to capture enough light from multiple camera sources that can be stitched together with software to produce incredibly real footage. The problem is that these cameras are priced at a high point and mostly end up in the hands of production giants. While you can submit a proposal to use/test one, it's highly unlikely that you can get your hands on one now unless you're willing to pay $30-$100K for them. With time, we expect the barrier to entry to be broken down as it usually is with next-gen camera tech.

Mid-tier cameras

Google Jump & Other 3D printed versions of it use 16 GoPro cameras and can record 4K high-quality live footage. The primary limit with this camera rig is the cost (16 GoPros which can add up) and there is no top and bottom view cameras – not a huge limit but still not as advanced as the high-tier cameras. We're talking the teens of thousands of dollars here.

Floor-tier cameras

There are a variety of camera rigs that use 3 or more GoPro cameras to capture 360-degree footage (lowering the overall price). Hero360 makes a variety of these. These can capture 4K footage but need more work on the production side as blind spots are solved for with advanced stitching. GoPro also announced a 5K VR camera named Fusion but has yet to share a release date or price. There is a plethora of other options in this tier emerging from Samsung, Garmin, 360fly, and more.

My take on video in VR:

The VR community is waiting for the software solution that fixes the "stitching" problem that comes with VR video production and the final VR product that's produced from these devices. For the producer, stitching the different scenes together with "real" accuracy is a convoluted process.

The stitching problem also accounts for the blurred or abnormally curved edges of the display, limiting the sense of "realism" for users. Take a few 360 degree experiences for a spin (pun intended) on your phone via YouTube and you'll get a feel for the stitching problem.

Beyond the stitching problem, 360 degree recording has it's own headaches for directors.

-Where does the director stand?
-Where does the boom mic go?

And more.

I'm sure before 2020, we will have clear solutions for all of the above but until then, we'll have to work with what we have.

4. Choose an Interaction Model

An Interaction model is an overarching set of design patterns that are consistent throughout an application. In VR, an interaction model evolves to define necessary constraints and frames up the possibilities of the interaction. There is a myriad of interaction models that are possible in VR, but I'll cover three primary ones that you can use as a starting point. The truth is that you can "make-up" interaction models based in sound design principles. Feel free to design your own from the ground up.

Start with character-view.

Start with whether or not your experience will be a first person, third person or some combination of the two views. Then build a model. Here are some model examples:

Grounded

In a "grounded" interaction model the user will be sitting, strapped in, standing still, or some variation of "set in place" for their experience. A lot of VR designers use this model because it's the least sickening right now and offers the lightest technical toiling. The grounded user is never to move even by force from another player – meaning if they are sitting in a wheelchair they are grounded as part of the experience but if that wheelchair moves that would be a hybrid grounded interaction model. Some VR designers insist that you provide a swivel chair for grounded experiences.

The Map

The user will move/transport throughout the experience with clear indicators of A to B and limitations outside of that path. This could be in the form of following someone, reading a map, reading cues, or more. They are told a clear story that they are to follow. While they can be curious and look anywhere, this model attempts to reduce curiosity in places that are not on the map. They may be able to touch and manipulate objects in the world as they come upon them in the map. A lot of games use this interaction model.

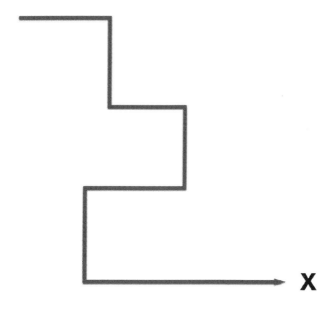

X

Free Me

The user will be able to move about freely (with apparent "position tracking" limitations) and will be able to interact directly with most objects. There is no clear map for the user to follow. This model is best for exploratory experiences.

5. Sketch and Storyboard

Start by sketching out your narrative. Take one sheet of paper or a big whiteboard and just draw some simple scenes, objects & the characters you want to build for the experience. If you plan on building an exploratory VR experience that won't have a chronologic order to it, this is a valuable step to narrow down what you want in the world.

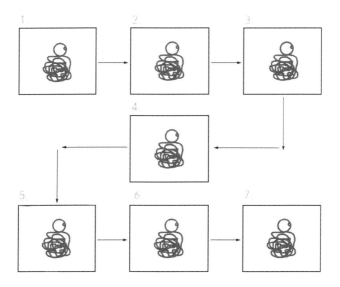

When done with your sketches – circle the ones that you feel are most important to the experience. Usually these are start/end scenes, climaxes (stop laughing at my word choice), important transitions, or parts that play a significant role in explaining the point. If you only drew "important" ones, then attempt to rank them with your own favorite ranking system ☺.

The un-circled or "lower ranked" will be areas that you could potentially cut corners if needed. This sketch sets the tone for time & resource commitment before a storyboard is even in place.

The storyboard is your wireframe.

Once you have sketched out a rough plan, it's time to start building the storyboard as you see it playing out in the virtual experience. (if your experience is exploratory (non-linear), you can settle for one giant board in the story or map the world out in boards that act as locations (unless there is a "point" you want the end user to reach, then it may still be helpful to have multiple shots).

For linear storytellers, you can plan to storyboard as you have in the past. Tell the experience as one would do in a movie/game/book but adapt it for virtual worlds. The boards can be anything that makes it easy for your team to prototype/build, but I recommend "block diagrams" like the one below

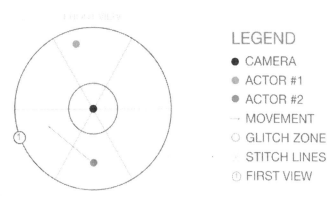

BLOCK DIAGRAMS

LEGEND
● CAMERA
● ACTOR #1
● ACTOR #2
--- MOVEMENT
○ GLITCH ZONE
STITCH LINES
① FIRST VIEW

I've found that the 360-degree block diagram is the easiest to design. If you have multiple rooms or one big plane that your experience lives on, you may want to have that be your first board. Then every board after that is a subsection of context for that first board, explaining the narrative and surroundings at that given point in the story.

The block diagram works for great for the designer that's trying to grasp the god's view of the world from the top down. For a more accurate storyboard, a designer could couple this with a first-person view by leveraging 360-panorama degree based graph paper. There's an awesome article on how to use this paper from Virtual Reality Pop – simply google *Virtual Reality Pop - Draw Sketches for Virtual Reality Like a Pro*

Sketch comfort zones.

You can also create your own comfort zones in each scene of the storyboard that focus on the areas you want to direct the user's attention. The comfort zone should enclose the views that are comfortable for the user to access across the x, y and z plane. (refer to the FOV headline under CONTENT later in this book for details)

6. Apply Sound, Cues, & Inputs

If you have designed video games in the past, then you are well aware that sound, cues and control inputs are an integral part of the experience and narrative. If you have designed for the computer/phone, you are probably used to taking wireframes or rough sketch designs right to the prototype/design stage. In VR, you have to consider sound, cues and control inputs across your storyboard. Here's why:

- Cues (depending on your story structure) could be the only thing keeping your story on track
- Sound is 50% of the user experience
- Control inputs are the medium through which the user interacts with the world you've created

Stamp on the Cues

Humans are innately more curious in a virtual environment than they are on a computer or phone. They want to look around and understand their surroundings first and foremost; then they want to see what they can play, move towards, or examine further. The only way you are going to get a human to follow a storyline is if you give them cues. Cues come in all different forms, below are just a few:

- Sounds (words, alarms, notifications, etc.)
- Lighting (tone, contrast)
- Environmental (roads, paths, walls, obstacles)
- Guides (arrows, lines, signs, clues)
- Outliers (pattern breakers, odd figures)

Examine your story from start to finish and draw in cues that you think will be helpful in getting them from board 1 to board 2. & board 2 to board 3, & so on.

I like to use a flashcard-like setup where I cut the storyboard out and write on the back of the board how a user will get from that board to the next.

You could also use "chains" and keep space between your boards for this step in the process and input cues across the chains that move between boards.

Sound Boards & Control Input Boards

Once you have the initial storyboard in order, Feel free to stamp on important sounds and critical control inputs. Not every sound or control input will be specific to a certain scene so feel free to create a separate board and sketch out universal sounds and input possibilities.

7. Develop the Test Plan

The testing phase in VR is where you earn your VR designer badge. While you may be familiar with collecting feedback for UX tests, VR testing involves new methods and perspectives that may take more time than traditional web/mobile user testing. Besides the obvious fact that the technology is new and unfamiliar to most people including yourself, you are testing "sub-reality" and how sound and comfortable that sub-reality is to the different persons using it.

Here is my formula for a solid VR UX test plan broken up into 10 parts:

1. Determine if you are trying to solve a problem, or entertain
2. The Standard (simulator sickness test)
3. Experience (navigation/controls)
4. Cognitive Map (ability to grasp concepts)
5. Advanced Tracking (biometrics, external video taping)
6. Rando Qualitative
7. Emotional Feedback
8. Did Your Solve Problem Or Entertain?

Determine if you're solving a problem or entertaining.

VR experiences will split into two primary categories – they will either solve a problem (teach, utility, therapy) for a particular set of people or they will entertain. Of course there are problem solvers that can entertain, but for the sake of testing you will want to focus on the core reasoning your narrative outlined in the beginning of the VR UX process. You don't have to build this into the test plan. Have the plan in mind when you are building out the test. Your choice will influence the types of test cases you want built in.

Standard Simulator Sickness Questionnaire (SSQ)

There was a simulator sickness questionnaire written in 1993, and it still stands as an excellent standard today for VR. It helps you quantify any physical/mental reactions from the experience. All of the credit for this questionnaire goes to the following

Kennedy, R. S., Lane, N. E., Berbaum, K. S., & Lilienthal, M. G. (1993). Simulator sickness questionnaire: An enhanced method for quantifying simulator sickness. *The International Journal of Aviation Psychology, 3(3)*, 203-220.

Here is an overview of the questionnaire.

Instructions : Circle how much each symptom below is affecting you <u>right now</u>.

1. General discomfort	<u>None</u>	<u>Slight</u>	<u>Moderate</u>	<u>Severe</u>
2. Fatigue	<u>None</u>	<u>Slight</u>	<u>Moderate</u>	<u>Severe</u>
3. Headache	<u>None</u>	<u>Slight</u>	<u>Moderate</u>	<u>Severe</u>
4. Eye strain	<u>None</u>	<u>Slight</u>	<u>Moderate</u>	<u>Severe</u>
5. Difficulty focusing	<u>None</u>	<u>Slight</u>	<u>Moderate</u>	<u>Severe</u>
6. Salivation increasing	<u>None</u>	<u>Slight</u>	<u>Moderate</u>	<u>Severe</u>
7. Sweating	<u>None</u>	<u>Slight</u>	<u>Moderate</u>	<u>Severe</u>
8. Nausea	<u>None</u>	<u>Slight</u>	<u>Moderate</u>	<u>Severe</u>
9. Difficulty concentrating	<u>None</u>	<u>Slight</u>	<u>Moderate</u>	<u>Severe</u>
10. « Fullness of the Head »	<u>None</u>	<u>Slight</u>	<u>Moderate</u>	<u>Severe</u>
11. Blurred vision	<u>None</u>	<u>Slight</u>	<u>Moderate</u>	<u>Severe</u>
12. Dizziness with eyes open	<u>None</u>	<u>Slight</u>	<u>Moderate</u>	<u>Severe</u>
13. Dizziness with eyes closed	<u>None</u>	<u>Slight</u>	<u>Moderate</u>	<u>Severe</u>
14. *Vertigo	<u>None</u>	<u>Slight</u>	<u>Moderate</u>	<u>Severe</u>
15. **Stomach awareness	<u>None</u>	<u>Slight</u>	<u>Moderate</u>	<u>Severe</u>
16. Burping	<u>None</u>	<u>Slight</u>	<u>Moderate</u>	<u>Severe</u>

You don't need to use this questionnaire to test sickness unless you need this level of detail. Usually, it's okay to simply test your experience and ask generally ask users about any sick feelings and when they occurred.

Experience (Navigation/Controls)

Time to validate the assumptions you had regarding your cues and control inputs.

You will be analyzing two primary parts of the interaction.

- The virtual interaction (how a user navigates your experience with their head and/or control inputs)
- The physical interaction (how comfortable are the inputs and interaction for the user)

I don't follow a particular format for this part of the testing phase. Rather, I mostly pay attention to the user's abstract feedback. I do pay attention to certain cues that I feel ahead of time may turn out to be difficult or new to the user, but those are merely preparatory assumptions.

Observe the experience inside the headset as well as the external tape and mark down cues or inputs that stood out (positively or negatively).

Finally, ask the user a simple question...

Was anything frustrating for you in regards to sound, controls or navigation?

Record their input & apply key notes to my sound, cue & input boards. After you collect feedback from a variety of testers, look at the whole experience and attack the areas with high frustration rates. There is no standard for what makes a high frustration rate, but I tend to lean on a 30% rule myself. If 30% of the users or more complain about or miss a cue or control, it should probably be revisited. Obviously, this % should be adapted depending on the # of testers you have.

Cognitive Map w/ Timing

Since most VR experiences give the user a newfound sense of freedom to look and do what they want, it's important that they grasped what you actually wanted them to do *and* in a reasonable amount of time. I like to pinpoint specific tasks in the storyboard and collect the time it took the user to get from task A to task B. I always include a "start" time point because the beginning of a VR experience is often where a user will be the most curious and therefore aimless.

Advanced Tracking

Because VR involves immersing a user's entire psyche and body into a new reality, we can do more advanced tracking involving the human body.

Biometrics involves tracking bodily reactions like heart rate, temperature, and more. There are a variety of devices you can purchase to track a human response based on biofeedback and it's quite interesting if you are designing an experience that emphasizes fear, empathy, or other emotional reactions.

Third person tracking involves a camera keeping track of the human body movements absent of the VR experience and world. This can be helpful when receiving feedback about the navigation or physical inputs involved in your experience.

Rando

This part of the testing experience needs no time in this book – it's simply you asking whatever questions you think are valuable to ensure your narrative dream becomes reality. You can ask it in any format you wish, and there are no rules. For example, I am working on an experience where I am trying to build in a feminist undertone – so I would ask participants if there was a social issue they felt the experience brought to light. If enough of them answered "feminism" or some form of it, I would grant a "passing grade" to that narrative goal. I call this part of the test process Rando (short for random questions).

Did You Solve the Problem and/or Entertain?

Coming full circle to the primary reason for your VR creation – you have to ask the tester in some way if you solved the problem for them or they whether or not they were entertained. It sounds simple, but this part of the test can be complicated depending on what you are trying to accomplish. For example, In building out EL A (a VR education project) I am trying to entertain the testers enough that they would buy a Google Cardboard or VR headset – strap it on a few times per week and watch a short informative video on whatever subject is being taught. Additionally, I want to get an understanding of how absorbable the content was and whether or not it taught them anything. ALSO – would they exchange their computer screen and YouTube videos for a learning experience in VR? All of these are the root of my business proposal, so I needed to make sure that I was accomplishing this on top of everything else I noted earlier for testing. I develop "scales" for this part of the test and weight out the answers but absolute "yes or no" questions would work too. The reason I use scales is that I am developing for multiple classes and will be doing so in the future, so I want to know which types of classes produce a higher score. Here are the questions I ask:

Scale 1
Were your entertained?

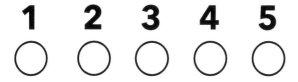

Scale 2
How Likely Are You To Use This Over Online Video for Learning?

Not Likely   Likely   Very Likely

Real-time testing feedback is not recommended.

Remember that people can't hear you when they're testing so don't design tests that require real-time feedback. Even if you speak through the earphones it will break the feeling of presence in the world and therefore create an unreliable result set. *DON'T BREAK PRESENCE!*

8. Prototype and Adjust the Strategy

I know sketching and storyboards are usually a pleasurable experience for designers. The not so pleasurable experience is creating the digital reality that follows. Digital work can be more efficient but can also present technical roadblocks and constraints that you don't have in free-hand design. The most important lesson I've learned in developing for VR is that you have to prototype before you finalize your UX strategy. Why? Because VR is in the early stages and the technology tends to limit more than it surprises with delight. Also, because the field is so new as a designer, you are encouraged to take risks and try new concepts. That's the beauty of a platform with little standards. Take risks and test them out in a prototype before you assume it will work for the general public. There's an upcoming section titled, *I Have New Interaction Ideas* where we will talk about this further.

Prototyping tools for VR have come a long way in one year's time but the field is still young. Here is a general overview of the prototyping tools in VR:

Game Engines

If you're already skilled in Unity or Unreal Engine then you could prototype inside these powerful engines. Since you've already overcome the learning curve, quick mockups will leverage the lower-end of your skillset. If you haven't worked in game engines before, you can still use these as a mockup tool but you may want to consider other options while you improve your game engine skill set.

The "Not" Game Engines

Here are some alternative mockup tools with easier learning curves:

A-Frame by Mozilla – a library for mocking up simple interactive experiences that people can test on their phones from anywhere. You can create these mockups on your desktop.

Google Blocks – you'll have to strap on an Oculus or Vive for Blocks. Mocking up 3D models in virtual reality may not be something you want to spend consecutive hours doing but this is a great program to quickly build an environment and analyze it from a 360 perspective. Using 6 primary tools (shape, stroke, paint, modify, grab and erase) you can mockup simple worlds.

Unity VR – While I've only seen it demoed (not for public use), Unity is working on an all-in-one VR designer tool similar to Blocks but with much more capabilities.

Build/Get 3D models for your prototype.

Google Blocks (already mentioned)

Gravity Sketch – you don't need CAD experience to start designing 3D models with Gravity Sketch. It's a straightforward tool attempting to simplify 3D modeling. You can upload your models to Sketchfab, where you can also buy a variety of 3D models made by others in the community.

TinkerCAD – is exactly what it sounds like. A tool for tinkering around with 3D model design. It's not nearly as complex as CAD so you can jump in and start designing quickly.

Blender - has won the hearts of many 3D model designers over the years but it's learning curve is steep. Don't let that scare you as models from Blender are how video games have been able to look so realistic the past few years.

Unity & Unreal Asset Library – you can find free 3D models or buy others in either of the two game engine libraries

I have new interaction ideas!

It's the perfect time in VR for a designer to take risks. With any new platform comes new ideas for interaction. Leap Motion created a 6 step process to consider when dreaming up new interactions:

1. *Tracking consistency* – ensure that the interaction is tracked consistently. There are a variety of limitations with controller tracking and even more with gestures. Input response and tracking are not always in sync so it's important to analyze the actual tracking data. You can use a diagnostic visualizer to do this (leap motion has one)
2. *Ease of detection* – are there obvious conditions to define the motion? Is the start and end of it obvious?
3. *Anticipate occlusion* – are there physical factors, like a bracelet blocking the user/input tracking to consider?
4. *Ergonomics* - is it comfortable for the user to perform once or many times?
5. *Position* – is it meant for VR experiences where the user is sitting down or standing? Both?
6. *Interaction overlap* – is it similar to other interactions in the world? You don't want a user in a position where the differences are so subtle that it's difficult for them to remember the difference

PART 2 – BEST PRACTICES

Before They Start

A VR experience will not be as self-prophesized as a phone/computer experience. The technology is new to most participants (have I said this before?), and you will need to not only guide them through the process of using the technology but also the personalization based on their physical attributes and preferences. Some of these decisions should be made by the user but most of them will be made by you based on your research and their attributes.

Adjust for player's experience.

How did you develop the person's character to play the experience? Standing, sitting, idle, moving, etc.

You may want to implement a feature in your experience that allows you to adjust for the player's height – especially if the player will be standing. If the height of the standing experience is not aligned with the height of the player, you run a higher risk that that person will have bodily identity distractions or feel sick while taking part. If the user is sitting down throughout the experience, you will decrease your chances that they will have an issue with height, but it's still something you want to include with the experience – you can remind the user to recenter their VR headset for their height before they start your experience.

Comfort settings.

We're not there yet, but with time, I'd anticipate that VR experiences ask a user some basic questions that will adjust the experience based on the user's comfort preferences. These will mostly be related to what I call "comfort settings." For example, the speed at which a player turns in the environment can vary. Many VR games give the player an option of turn speed because it's been shown that rapid turns help alleviate motion sickness for users that are prone to it.

As more basic question/answer combos are backed by science, experience comfort settings will become a basic part of the user flow.

Outside of standard comfort settings, there will be additional comfort settings specific to the world. For instance, if an experience consisted mostly of playing a virtual drumset, the player should have the option to adjust the placement and height of the various kit pieces to their liking.

The avatar.

We all like to be someone else from time to time. That's the beauty of living through a character in a book, film or play. However, there's always been a clear physical separation between you and the character. In VR, that separation is thin so you may want to consider giving the player control over their avatar's features. Why? Because some people feel uncomfortable being "in" a body that doesn't resemble their own. Giving them control over their avatar's gender, skin color, body type, height (perspective), clothes and more will ensure they have as little body dysmorphia as possible. On the flipside it will give them an opportunity to experience different body types. It's not always negative folks!

Build in an intro tutorial.

Think of the basic tutorial as a mandatory introduction to the basic components below

- Controller inputs (gestures, buttons)
- Movement (are there teleportation inputs, speed changes, etc.)
- Object interaction (the dos and don'ts of the virtual world)

Dos and don'ts of my virtual world.

Players will attempt to interact with your virtual world like they do with the physical. There will obviously be affordances that exist in the real world that won't apply to yours. If there is something the user can't do that they would otherwise expect to be "doable" then feel free to tell them ahead of time and let them down easy. This will reduce the amount of time they spend to figure out your world and reduce the number of affordance surprises. For example, if you design a floor with a bunch of rocks and the rocks are small enough that they look like they can be picked up – but you didn't design them to be picked up, then you could tell the user ahead of time, *no rocks can be interacted with.*

This is more important in VR than it was in gaming or the web because time was not correlated with comfort. In VR, the more time a person spends in the experience the more prone they are to discomfort and sickness so best to educate the user on dos and don'ts ahead of time.

Warn the user.

VR is more personal than other mediums so it's important to warn users of any content that may be too intense for them. Because of this, you may want to warn the user of any strong feelings that may come – fear, anxiety, pain, etc. If your content has an age requirement you'll want to make sure you ask for that. If your content contains graphic material you'll want to notify the participant that they will be exposed to it and the nature of what it is.

Decide on 1st Person or 3rd Person.

You can put your user in a virtual world that they control from a first-person point of view or the play could be following a player from a third-person point of view. Most experiences thus far in VR are from a first person POV. Either way, give the player a heads up on the perspective they will be assuming. (we'll talk more about this in the section titled *Storytelling*)

Do not start your experience until they push the start button.

Give explicit user instructions on how to start the experience. And make the start button clear. You want to have a splash page before they start, so they are not thrown into an immersive experience before they are reading. It may be a good time to share the pause/exit button as well.

Give "familiar" time.

When a user straps on the VR headset, they should not be rushed into committing an action. They should be granted the freedom to look around and get familiar with their surroundings. In my testing, I've concluded that 20 seconds is usually enough time to achieve this but it's completely dependent on the world and narrative.

Length of time.

Notify the user of the duration of time the experience will take. If an experience is longer than 20 minutes you may want to give the user breaks or notify them of the length so they can build in their own breaks. Either way, a general rule of thumb for the human eye is no more than 20 straight minutes in front of a screen.

The soft lead in.

It's best practice to gradually unveil your virtual world. Soft lead ins using music with a subtle crescendo combined with creeping light exposure can make for a good start that will please the user. An abrupt start with bright visuals or piercing sounds will be jarring.

Give starter cues.

Since there is 360 degrees of space to experience, a user will not know where to start unless there is an obvious cue. That cue can come in the form of a sound, secluded object, narrow light path, small arrows indicating directions or many other forms of indicators that we see in everyday life – like road signs, etc. Text is a possibility here but the consensus in the VR world right now is the less reading the better – as words are difficult on the eye over extended periods of time in VR.

MOVEMENT

Create a Movement Model

Movement models will ground your experience with clear constraints built in. A movement model describes how you want a user to move around your VR space. Your model could consist of one basic user movement such as walking at a steady pace on their own command, or it could consist of multiple moves throughout an experience like walking at a steady pace, running, riding an elevator, sitting down, backing up, flying, etc.

You can overlay the movement model on your storyboard. Why? It's important to see the player movements as an outline in VR because you can break down these important motion changes for improvement and adjustments. For example, you may play through your experience and discover that it makes you sick. With a movement model in place, you can identify each movement mode or combination as a potential culprit as part of the whole. Without a movement model, you may end up focusing on one movement when in reality it was the combination and order of two modes that eventually lead to the sickness. It also helps you digest user feedback more quickly because you are familiar with their all movement possibilities.

Know the 6 degrees of freedom (6 DOF).

The body has 6 different ways of moving in space. It can rotate and translate in XYZ. The device used by a VR participant will use orientation tracking to determine how many degrees of freedom the user is granted. Phone-based VR experiences are using 3 DOF meaning that a user can look up/down, left/right, forward/backward. The Oculus, Vive and PlayStation VR headsets us 6 DOF (+X, -X,+Y,-Y,+Z,-Z) which allows for the same 3 DOF movements PLUS rotation around those axes. Once you select your VR tech and tools (step 2), you will know how much movement you can leverage. It's important to note the limitation if you decide on a VR phone experience.

You can couple either of these freedom rules with "manipulation" which means you can also manipulate objects in the space with the "x" degrees of freedom.

The core VR movement rules:

- Forwards is better than Backwards
- Up/Down is better than Strafe Left/Right
- A fast camera cut is better than a gentle camera rotation

Place the camera right above the avatar's neck.

Make sure that the camera view is right above the neck of the avatar – don't mess with putting a camera at the leg-level of a user or something odd like that.

People get sick when movement is done wrong.

The number one complaint from VR testing is that the user experiences motion sickness. It can ruin the experience for some testers indefinitely. So it's important to understand that most of VR's best practices came about from understanding how to avoid sickness. Often, it's the conflict between visual and bodily senses that is to blame.

People get confused when movement is done wrong.

While it causes sickness most of the time, body confusion is another setback for the VR user when taking on an experience that gets movement wrong. You should never decouple user and camera movements. Since the VR experience is most similar to the human experience, it's much more sensitive to throwing people "off" if the virtual view is not aligned with how they move their body & relational objects in the real-world.

The most comfortable VR experiences involve little to no movement.

This statement comes from Oculus and their intensive research so keep it in mind as you build for VR. This may change as the tech evolves.

Have head-tracking enabled at all times.

A new development in UX that becomes evident and important is head-tracking. Head-tracking enables objects to stay in a fixed position regardless of how the user moves their head. There are exceptions to the fixed position rule that we will talk about later in the "content" section. All VR apps should enable head-tracking at all times during the experience. Even a short pause can cause disorientation. There are small exceptions to this rule – if your experience needs a moment to load the next world there are times where the load screen could have head tracking turned off – for instance – if it fades to black and the user can't see anything anyways - In that case, it wouldn't make sense to keep motion tracking enabled.

It's possible that head-tracking (position tracking) could be lost while playing – it's smart to have a warning popup if the device recognizes this as the experience is ruined if tracking is lost where it should be active.

For most VR devices, head-tracking is a prerequisite to have your experience featured.

Let the user drive.

The player should be an active driver rather than a passenger when it comes to camera motion. Regardless of which narrative person their character viewing form, give them a "degree of control." This control of their viewing experience reduces the chance of motion sickness. Much like driving a car is better than being a passenger on winding roads.

You should design most of the experience in a way that accounts for them to be able to look at any of the 6 DOF. While it makes sense that a user should be given control, there are plenty of tests that have shown instances where they shouldn't, and they usually involve set motion. For example, a roller coaster experience may be a fixed motion experience where you maintain a particular cone-of-focus because there is already a hefty amount of motion taking place. If a user adds head movement in addition to that motion it can cause sickness. If you plan to take the user on a mobile journey like a boat, car, plane, etc. it's important that the speed of that journey determines whether or not it's comfortable to give them full camera control.

There are other times where you may want to focus their attention on one particular thing and lock their camera motion to that thing – IF you plan to do this, you must warn them that the rest of their view will be blacked-out or out of view. You can do this with sound cues or a simple popup. I recommend that most of your experience allows the user to control the camera as most of my user testing has shown this to be most enjoyable and awe-inspiring.

Human bodies move more in arcs than in straight lines

In a 3D space, you'll have to account for the slight arc that every human naturally embodies when they move. Having head-tracking will solve for this but if you are controlling the camera view, keep in mind that every person walks with a slight arc.

Don't accelerate or decelerate often.

Use acceleration sparingly. When you use it, make it near instantaneous and as short as possible. Give the user control of accelerations as often as you can.

If you move, make the speed constant.

Use a constant velocity when the player is moving. Sudden speed changes can cause sickness. For example, when you fly – you feel the takeoff and the drop to the landing but most of the flight experience you feel very little because the plane is flying at a more constant velocity which is more comfortable to you the passenger. Humans move at an average of 1.4m/s. You can give the user control over a speed change (i.e. walking to running away from a monster)

Encourage neck movements.

Right now, VR tech relies on a light but real headpiece that will inevitably add weight to your head that your neck will have to support. You want to encourage neck movements in your experience to extend the range of motion and keep the neck comfortable. There's a happy medium between too much and too little that you will have to figure out when testing. Naturally, a user will want to look around, but it doesn't hurt to have built-in movement commands to encourage it at times where they have been locked into a stable view for some time. A good example of this was seen in the Eve Valkyrie Demo at the Oculus Announcement last year when the commander asked the central player to "check their 6" meaning "look behind you."

Teleportation is cool but sickening when not done right.

Teleportation can be a great alternative to walking from one location to another but it can be disorienting for the user if they are suddenly transported to a completely new orientation. If you choose to teleport, make sure that your user is ready for this by prepping them to stand still, try to preserve their original orientation. Provide them with visual cues to make them comfortable in their new location and experiment with fading techniques to find the least fatiguing/sickening transition.

Don't rotate the user's view when teleporting as this can be uncomfortable.

It doesn't always have to be a "new" location. Teleportation can also mean moving to a distant location that's already visible to the user. If it's in the distance it's important to use a frame of reference that will orient them quickly once in the new location. Some designers display the near-scale of the object they are pointing at in the distance before teleportation is induced and it's been shown to help smooth the transition.

God view.

Allowing a player to enter third-person "God Mode" is another take on movement that isn't teleportation. This view gives them a high view of their avatar and the world as they move their avatar from one part of the world to another. Once settled into the new location, they can ease back into the first-person view and explore.

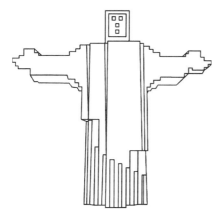

Don't zoom in or out quickly.

This already stated but focused on user movement (acceleration). Zooming is essentially the same as acceleration and therefore adheres to the same rules.

No sudden changes in direction, please.

If you modify the course of the experience without apparent warning or let it happen too quickly, you are going to disorient the user's perception of the scene. Momentarily, You can warn the user and fade to black if you plan on doing such changes. Rapid Movement next to objects is also a bad idea – causes the same feeling of disorientation and blur.

Less backwards & side-to-side.

Not to restate what I've already stated but the less you make a player move, the better. If you have a large room where a user will be walking around with a decent amount of position tracking volume than sure, you can include these movements in more of your experience. But if you are designing for a stationary experience moving your avatar back and sideways while your genuine body remains stationary can feel odd to the user and cause bodily confusion and/or sickness. We almost never move back or side-to-side in real life so it would feel strange even if we did move our bodies that way with the virtual experience tracking. That being said, there are situations where stepping back and moving from side to side would be easier than twisting or turning to complete a movement so I'm not saying NEVER allow the user to move back or side-to-side - just consider doing it less.

Move in constant lines more than turning.

Traditionally, video games rely on first-person views to navigate never-ending mazes within levels that contain a variety of corners, crevices, stairs, and curves. In VR, the less turning, the better for prolonged comfort.

Some VR creators have instituted a 30-degree instantaneous turn (snap turn) when the user presses left and right turn buttons to avoid the gradual movement on turns – this jump has proven to be less sickening for the user but is not something they understand intuitively straightaway. The popular horror game Dreadhalls was incredibly sickening for me until I selected the "quick turn" option for all the dungeon corners.

Snap turns.

Because we are dealing with 360 degrees, it makes sense that turning is a common motion. If motion sickness and fatigue time are an issue for your experience you can use *snap turns* (mentioned above) instead of gradual turns and limit the amount of hard turns overall. Snap turns speed up the organic turn time of human motion so that it happens quickly. Experiment with turning times as you test. You can set turn speed in the settings of the game engine.

Speed is a virtue.

The speed at which a player is allowed to move should be similar to the speed of natural human movement (walking or light job) or slower depending on your tests - even if the character is not human. Unreal Engine made a comment that they cut the video game speed of a character by 1/3 for VR to make it feel comfortable and more human-like than what you are used to in a video game.

Build stationary environments for stationary moments.

If the user is meant to be stationary during gameplay, it's best practice to build a virtual setting for that state. Give them a chair to sit in, strap them into a cockpit, glue them to the floor, etc. These settings will help them reconcile the sensation of movement in VR. Vection will occur when the player's vision tells them they are moving through space but their body tells them they are sitting in a chair.

Lagging content will feel awful & unrealistic

High-tier VR devices rely on the power of a computer tower because they need to show high-powered realistic graphics with very little call and response lag time. What's an acceptable lag? Best practice right now is surely under 100 milliseconds with 20 milliseconds being the golden target. In human tests, results vary on when they notice the lag as some humans can detect as little as 3 ms of lag and others don't even notice 100 ms. Your best bet is to test your experience with multiple users of varying ages, genders, and vision.

The rift has a built-in latency tester that you can leverage if you are creating for the platform. Oculus refers to latency as the amount of time between a user's movement and when the image shows on the screen. You may hear VR folks call it "motion-to-photon" as well. You can reduce latency with Oculus by implementing "predictive tracking" code which predicts where a user will be looking or going next and renders that information ahead of time.

Tech targets to avoid lagging content.

Frames Per Second (fps) = frames per second that are rendered by the software

Anything lower than 60 fps will feel unrealistic to the user. As systems stand now, you can cut back on things like dynamic shadows, dynamic lights and aggressive radius attenuation to improve the fps. It should be consistent throughout the experience.

Disply Refresh Rate = times per second the display refreshes. Minimum display rate is 6ohz and an optimal target is 10ohz

Sample Rate = times per second is the positional tracking data of the headset sampled. ~100hz minimum with an optimal target of 1000hz. A poor sample rate has been a primary culprit for motion sickness.

Haptic feedback & distance.

Haptic feedback can be used to inform a player on how close or far away they are from a particular object. It can guide their movement by acting as an annoying barrier as well. A tough rumble tends to feel alarming to the user and a light vibration feels like they are on the verge of something – increasing the strength of the feedback as they close in.

Tiresome motions.

A player should not be asked to perform a motion or movement that is difficult at first try but more importantly, one that could tire them out over time. For example, asking a player to keep their arms extended holding something above their head = super uncomfortable after a few seconds.

Objects in Motion.

Avoid having moving objects take up a large share of the user's view. This will likely cause "self-motion" which makes the player feel like they are moving, when in fact, they're not.

Avoid Dizzy Bat

Dizzy Bat is when the body rotates on one axis at a time that the head is tilted. This condition will most likely cause sickness.

Don't intentionally design for spins & other sickening crap.

Don't design environments that encourage lots of spinning, or repetitive actions in on place. Never intend to sicken the user.

Children ages 2-12 are more likely to experience sickness. Consider this if designing for children.

Position tracking allows for more user exploration.

Keep in mind as you design for VR that the user can look around, under, on top of and more. Technically speaking, a user can put their head through objects in a virtual world. Oculus has found that users tend to avoid doing this unless the game instructs them to do so. If your objects allow for a user to move "through" you may want to have a prompt ready that allows them to readjust their position in case the camera view through the objects disorients them.

Position tracking volume has its limits. Make sure that you warn a user well in advance of reaching those limits so they are not offset by the camera experience that may take place in response to reaching the limits. Oculus recommends that if a user is about to lose position tracking, you should fade the view to black as it's less jarring than the view with lost position tracking.

Slopes & steps should be used at angles that don't upset one's stomach.

For now, slopes and steps can be used but try to avoid steepness. If your steps/slopes are too steep, they can produce a feeling of "falling off" which can make a user feel like their stomach is dropping. Avoid overusing slopes and steps. Ramps tend to bed more comfortable for users as the horizontal edges of steps can cause vection because you are not physically stepping on the stairs.

Accessibility & VR.

VR has already proven to be an interesting health accompaniment. There's been uplifting stories of how it's helped curb depression in serious burn victims and aided in the recovery of PTSD patients. The realism that comes with the medium makes it a perfect fit for allowing humans to experience things that their body may not allow for.

Outside of being a health accompaniment, accessibility for all body types needs to be considered.

Here are some of the "modes" to think about for accessibility:

1. Physical/Motor skills – movement of arms, legs and neck to accomplish a task. As well as standing vs. sitting. You may want to account for body limitations, injuries, wheelchairs and more
2. Hearing loss – this is especially important for mood and sound cues. You may want a version of the experience that doesn't rely on sound cues but strictly visual
3. Sight – perhaps give users the ability to control the size of text and important objects in the world. There isn't a brail for VR yet to account for blind individuals but perhaps using haptic technology alone, someone will dream up an interesting sub-reality story that's categorized as VR
4. Photosensitive Epilepsy – very rare but account for it in your warnings. If you aren't aware, PE individuals are prone to seizures so they don't respond well to an overstimulation of lights

SOUND

50%

Sound is 50% of the VR experience.

You can develop the most beautiful VR world known to woman but if your sound sucks *it* will ultimately suck. It's important that you test audio cues much like you test visuals and movements. Right now, there are few standards when it comes to VR sound cues – there will surely be some as more people use the technology and develop for it.

Sound should come from headphones.

It may seem like a no-brainer, but unlike the web/mobile VR will always rely on headphones for the auditory experience (for now). Headphones ensure that your ears are properaly immersed in the world with the rest of your head. I say "properly" because VR sound uses a head-related transfer function (HRTF) to translate a sound with a fixed position in the world to the sound experienced by both of your ears. Oculus uses HRTF designed to account for sounds bouncing off your head, shoulders, torso and inner ears.

Use binaural sound cues & recordings.

The easiest way to explain binaural sound is that it's recorded and input in a way that reflects real human hearing so when you hear something coming from behind you on your left side you will hear more of that activity in your left ear, and it will be fainter in your right ear. Picture a binaural microphone to have the shape of a human head.

It's common sense on why this is important – if a user hears a sound that doesn't match a typical human experience in a world that feels like a human experience, it will cause confusion and sound unrealistic.

When recording sounds for your design, you will want to use an ambisonic microphone. It records a complete sound file that can be decoded to a binaural audio format.

Spatialize the audio of other virtual characters that speak.

If you pipe in the sound of talking characters over a central audio channel or simply left/right, it can produce unrealistic sound. Always attempt to spatialize sound and align it to the directions the characters face and their position. The same holds true for objects or menu items that make noise.

Real-life sounds are more impactful than designed ones

This statement is somewhat subjective but thus far it's true. Do your best to record real-life sounds even if you are building a digital environment that mocks the real world.

Don't break sound expectations.

If a bird noise comes from below, it's quite possible that a user will still look up. Why? Because in the real world most birds are up. Do your best to avoid breaking one's expectations of real-world sounds and their likely position, meaning, etc.

Adjust sounds with movement.

If a player moves further away from an object making noise, then the noise should dim depending on their distance from that object. Consider using the doppler effect for this relationship.

Same goes for turns. Google created an experience called Tabel where they placed the user in the middle of a restaurant surrounded by 6 different tables, each with their own set of people. As a viewer, I had control over which table conversation I wanted to hear by moving my chair to face the table. As I moved in a circle, conversations that I moved away from naturally faded into the distance and ones that I moved to view came through clearer and louder.

Avoid invisible or unidentifiable sounds.

Unless you are trying to confuse the player. Sound cues are so important in VR that your player will almost always try to respond to an isolated sound.

CONTENT

Field of view (FOV).

It's important to understand that there are two views when a virtual experience is taking place. There is the Display-Field-Of-View (dFOV) which means the field that the user can see without distortion, it's what they are looking at (also known as a cone-of-focus), and Camera-Field-Of-View (cFOV) which is the full spectrum seen by the rendering cameras of what is on the screen but not all of it is in focus for the user.

Because there is more screenspace than the eye can behold at a given point in time, it's important to understand the constraints. The dFOV for a player is about 94 degrees.

Moving Left/Right
They can move left or right comfortably another 30 or so. Mid-level comfort from 30-55 and difficult from 55+.

Moving Up/Down
Users can comfortably move <=20 degrees up and 12 degrees down. Mid-level comfort from 21-60 degrees for looking up and 13-40 degrees for looking down.

Now that we know this, all the key elements that are critical to the experience/gameplay should be within ~30 degrees of the user's view. Non-critical but necessary elements should be within ~60 degrees.

Create a content map.

Similar to the movement model, you may want to create a content map that calls out important moments in the user experience where content is critical; this includes but is not limited to instructions, warnings, signs, valuable text, & helpful images. Again, this will help you narrow down relationships in your test phase so you can learn from each one or their collective results.

Don't condense too much content in one place.

Keep the density lower than what we are used to seeing on a computer/phone screen. You don't need to have it all in the cone-of-focus as a user can move their head and explore. Keep words spread out within reason.

Avoid presenting two different images to each eye.

Since a VR headset technically shows two pictures of the scene to two different eyes, it's important that those images are the same and only different regarding viewpoint. Even if the images are similar, and only their lighting is different, it will distort the view.

Don't rush content.

VR is an exploratory medium. Give the user more time to acclimate than you would in a video game or on the web. As we stated before, give them at least 15-20 to figure out their new surroundings.

Leave room for the holy spirit.

Keep UI's & popup content 2-3 meters away from the user. You'll want to maintain a comfortable distance between the viewer and the layered virtual objects at the onset of their view or throughout the experience if you plan to have them stationary. If they are too close, it can distort the view. Leap Motion came up with a solution for this issue applying a "force away" from the viewport to repel nodes to a comfortable distance.

The Z axis.

If something is 20 meters or beyond, the human eye doesn't see much stereo separation so you'll want to keep critical details within that range (the unit of measurement varies depending on the dev engine you're using). Anything that is 0.5 meters or closer is too close and will cause eye strain - most will go cross-eyed. You will want to increase this number by a bit for text since a user has to move across the plane with ease.

A UI should take up 1/3 or less of the cone of focus.

You'll want the user to use their eyes as little as possible when interacting with a UI, so it's important that you try to center it for them and cover enough but no more than 1/3 of the visible screen space.

Apply persistent UI content to objects in the 3D space rather than floating.

If you are playing a game that contains a "life count" you will want to be able to reference that life count as you play. In VR, you could put the life count on the users hand if they are using "touch" controls. A watch, for example, could contain all the vitals you need much like in the real-world. If you are not using touch, you could apply it to any object being carried by the first-person user or another character's back if you are following someone.

Active objects should be reactive before the user takes action.

In most cases, not every object in your VR space will be interactive. Some items will be disabled from interaction and instead of the user having to go through the entire input only to be let down, you can provide them with some kind of indicator, confirming the object is selectable.

Load screens & warnings.

Much like the web and gaming, you will want to notify the user if content is still loading or if they are attempting to do something that is not allowed. For loading, you can fade to black but give the user an audio cue that you will be doing so. For loading text and warnings, be sure not to fix them to the middle of the screen but rather to the middle of their cone of focus through the use of head-tracking. If the user is trying to complete a move with a gesture of some sort you can align it with their gesture inputs.

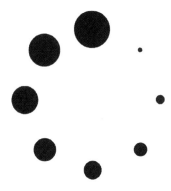

Display a recticle or leading line for fine targeting tasks.

A recticle is a visual aid to track targets – when active, you should project a light source or design apparent hover states. Make sure the recticle is drawn at the same depth as the object it is tracking or you run the risk of it appearing as a doubled image confusing the human eye. Oculus refers to this as "ray-casting" and recommends that you have an explicit targeting cursor rendered at the depth of the object it is targeting along with adequate feedback that what you are targeting is responding. Feedback can be done with lighting, animation, etc.

A common practice that's being used in recticle design is to increase the size of a recticle with distance. The further away you are from a target the more ground the recticle should cover.

For selection with a recticle, the best practice is to take the user's gaze and an input device as a means of selection vs. head movements. Head nods to indicate a "selection" can result in motion sickness because they increase the possibility of a user's head tilting off axis, which can lead to an effect called dizzy bat or "pseudo coriolis effect"

3D is better than 2D for complex data sets.

Depth is your friend when it comes to showing data sets in VR. Instead of arranging data sets on a 2D plane add depth and layer them for the user to delve through.

Displaying options of choice.

You don't want to display choice on a 2D surface like that of shelves in a shopping aisle, rely on 3D layering, shading & depth. Netflix designed an interface that still prioritizes what they think is relevant to you by bringing it closer to you than the other choices and shading it a bit brighter with more contrast than the choices that lie behind it.

Curve written content & menus.

When displaying text, it works best on a curve and with depth. The text shouldn't be close to the face of the user but rather at a distance making it easier to see and consume. Don't make them read too much though, as VR is not a reading platform (yet). Feel free to rely on audio for cases you would have put in text on a mobile/web page.

Menus are easier to analyze as curved walls of text & art. Don't mix 2D menus with 3D as it's jarring for the user.

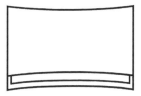

Keep the horizon line steady.

Don't let the horizon line shiver or roll – on a ship, a rolling horizon makes you sick so don't expect this to be different in a VR experience.

Altitude matters.

Try to avoid having the user's point-of-view so low that the ground is always changing as they move. It can lead to intense motion exposure that will fatigue and/or sicken the user.

Independent visual backgrounds can reduce discomfort.

One method that has been tested and proven to work for individuals that have issues with simulator sickness is the use of independent visual backgrounds. These backgrounds remain stationary while the rest of the experience is moving. An example of this would be a cloud that could hang up in the sky in the distance that's stable and never-changing – it still looks real, and the rest of the experience is moving but having that stable cloud seems to help people feel less sick and more grounded.

Oculus tested the use of a lined grid system that shows the distance of the "space's borders" and found it to be a positive adjustment. There are obviously rooms and experiences where it wouldn't make sense to have a cloud or other object off in the distance – think in a house or anywhere indoors for that matter. This grid-based system does suspend belief a bit but can make a huge difference in comfort – it's up to you to determine if it's necessary for your experience.

Don't rumble or head bob.

You should not treat errors, crashes and hitting a wall as you do on screens today – with a rumble, shake or bright light. Rumbling and shaking can make a user sick and abrupt bright light is jarring. A lot of video games use head bopping to simulate the motion of walking but this won't be as comfortable in VR as every bop is technically acceleration that can wear on a user.

Objects that avatars are holding in first person view shouldn't be big and visible when not In use.

Generally speaking, first-person games allow the primary character to carry objects like weapons, goods, etc. Sometimes these objects usually appear in the bottom of the view and take up a small amount of screen space. However, in stereoscopic view, these objects will be at the forefront if shown near the bottom of the screen and this can force the user to make large changes in eye convergence = not comfortable. Here are a few thoughts you can test:

- Avoid showing the object in the first person view
- Only show the object when in use or absolutely necessary
- Sometimes a very faint version of the object with dark and clear contrast takes some of the strain away
- Some have tried to make the object 2D instead of 3D, and it has lessened the eye strain

Avoid flicker.

Users are highly sensitive to flicker or strobing in virtual environments and it is advised that you don't design large objects that flicker or full-screen flickers as you build. These can be very discomforting to the end user experience.

Beware of strong+repetitive object motion.

You don't want to place moving objects in the environment that consumes view space and in constant motion. An excellent example of this is a train that never ends. If that train is tracking across the screen and always in motion, it will eventually wear on the user. The solution is to build a short train that will pass in a short amount of time.

Fade to black & never white

Some movies, games and videos will fade to white when transitioning to the ensuing screen or closing. Fade to black in VR. It's more comfortable than white.

Use pattern recognition.

Use pattern recognition to guide users through an experience. When one looks at a row of objects and all of the objects are the same except for one they will be curious about the outlier. You can use this trick to guide a user to a particular place in the experience. Gaming has used this since its inception.

With that in mind, humans learn best with pattern recognition breaks down. Work with illusions to teach.

Use contrast.

Contrast rules still apply (big, small, bright, dark, etc.). Humans are more likely to approach a dark contrast with ease than light (except warning light), and you can use this rule for attention cues. Bright objects in a scene have been shown to discomfort sensitive users and cause eye strain, so if your experience is causing fatigue, it's possible you need to dim the brights.

Hands dysmorphia.

While most VR experiences leverage a controller, it's common for a user's hands to be in view. Obviously these are virtual hands and therefore not the actual hands of the user. While it's not a significant problem, some users have reported feeling more comfortable and less distracted by their hands if you give them something topical to place on their hands. Light gloves are a good example. The virtual hands don't even need to be bearing gloves, it's more about the user feeling like their hands have external qualities.

More about menus.

Similar to the early days of web, menus come in a variety of different shapes, sizes and places. When it comes to shuffling of items within the menu there are a few options to consider:

Progressive Linear or Orbital
Menu items are grouped where the user can see the next item aligned on the right and/or left side of the selected item or top/bottom. When moving between items, the menu orbits around its central point. Usually depth and space (45 degree angle line and progressively smaller for each subsequent item) are taken into account for this sort of setup.

Idle Call & Point
Menu setup uses two controllers and the menu is stationary with no moving items. The user will call open the menu with one of the remotes. Usually this menu will be directly attached to the remote that's called open the menu the player will use the other remote to navigate the menu and select.

The Box
The box menu has a menu item on each face of the box and it rotates around its central axis for navigation. This tends to work well if you have at least four and less than eight menu items to choose from.

Eye the target.

If your experience involves repetitive maneuvering that requires targeting, you should consider handing the user a piece of common sense real-world advice they may omit from memory inside the virtual headset…closing one eye tends to improve targeting accuracy. Feel free to prompt them with this in the intro tutorial or if they pass a threshold (set by you) for targeting problems.

Design beautifully but know performance is queen.

One of the primary hurdles that designers new to VR will have to overcome is the discrepancy between what they want to design and what can be beautifully rendered in the virtual environment without causing latency/lagging issues.

Object weight may be annoying.

Early user feedback on experiences that try to vary the weight of interactive objects in the world with leading lines or other indicators have been described as "annoying" vs. objects simply being without a weight indicator.

Blocks > than blades.

If you are designing a VR experience with a Game Engine, be aware that large block objects look better than skinny objects right now. That's precisely why Google named their builder Blocks!

The floor.

You must include a floor/ground in your virtual world or your user will be disoriented and may feel as if they are falling indefinitely. In his book *The Ecological Approach to Visual Perception*, James J. Gibson breaks down the primary terrain features to think about when designing a virtual world.

Ground
The ground is usually not open and allows for balanced locomotion.

Path
Affects the pedestrian motion from one place to another.

Obstacle
A relatively-sized object that affords collision.

Barrier
Similar to an obstacle in that it's an object, but blocks a pathway.

Water Margin
Prevents pedestrian locomotion via water or other natural sources.

Step
Supports both ascent and descent.

Slope
Same as a step but may not support movement entirely, depending on the slope.

CONTROL INPUTS

Standards are forming.

In the first edition of this book, I concluded that standards were not in place because controllers were in their infancy. 2 years on and we have some standardization in the "types" of remotes that exist but the input mapping for those remotes is still quite wild.

Some standard assignments have been set. There's usually a button assigned for:

- Trackpad/Joystick for movement
- Menu/Home
- Select
- Volume

As a VR designer it's important to understand the options you have in regards to control inputs because they are such a critical part of the UX.

High-tier device controls:

Oculus

two controllers (one for each hand) both feature a joystick for movement, trigger and x & y buttons that you can map.

HTC Vive

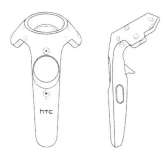

features a trackpad for movement that can be pressed along with a menu button and system button that you can map. There is also a grip button on the side and trigger button placed on the back.

Playstation VR

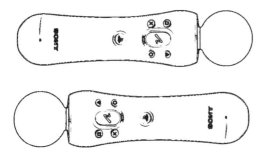

two wands that mimic the functionally of Nintendo wii remotes. Features a home button and four lettered buttons that you can map much like the playstation controller.

Mid-tier device controls:

Samsung Gear

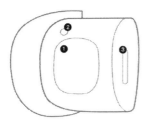

1. volume +/-
2. trackpad – movements
3. back

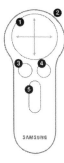

1. trackpad – movements
2. trigger
3. back
4. home
5. volume +/-

Google Daydream

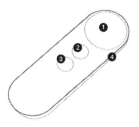

1. **trackpad – movements**
2. varies by app (menu, back, etc.)
3. home
4. volume +/-

Floor-tier device controls:

Google Cardboard

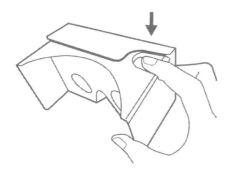

features one magnetic input button that is most often mapped to "selection" in a mobile VR experience.

Users can't see the input device.

It's important to note that unlike other media platforms, VR users can't physically see the input device. Most VR designers have solved for this by projecting the real-world controller into the virtual experience but even then, details of the controller may be out of sight for the user. You'll have to figure out if it makes sense to show the controllers in your experience or account for the blind hand in the form of training.

Your tutorial should explain controls.

Once you've decided on the final controller inputs for your experience, you should have a section in your tutorial the features the mappings. It should also be available in the menu throughout the experience.

Be aware of occlusion.

If you've designed for the Nintendo Wii, Xbox Kinect or Leap Motion, you know exactly what I'm talking about. VR controls are reliant on a single sensor or multiple sensors placed about the room. Most of these sensors use light to detect movements. Occlusion is when an object (in most cases) blocks light from a call+answer interaction between the control inputs and the receiver. I say "be aware" because there are all kinds of issues that can be prevented with a simple design tweak or warning. If long baggy sleeves are the "hot" fashion item for women and you design the experience for women, some are likely to have a bad experience because their sleeves got in the way of their hand input. I could list off thousands of examples but I'd prefer to keep the book short so that I can keep the cost down for you ☺. Speaking of cost, Time for a plug - *f&$k student loans! I'm not bitter. Okay, I'm bitter* ☺.

Press any key to recenter.

There are many VR experiences that take full control of a user's visual plane. It's important that you allow them to recenter the headset before starting and leave it as an option at any point in the experience. Also, since their vision is impaired from the real world, you should give them a myriad of buttons to push in order for this command to take action. (Oculus source of information)

Keep controls simple.

It seems like common sense, but it's hard to hold back in VR development because of all the new possibilities. The best VR experiences to date have simple control inputs and don't overcomplicate with new gestures, odd button combinations, etc. Light controls dramatically reduce the player fatigue and the more time you give them to explore the content the longer they will stay in.

Fuse.

Fuse is an input that allows a user to look-to-select = If they stare at something with a recticle guide for a certain period of time, they imply a selection. Google Cardboard has experiences where the user can either push the side button or fuse. The only issue with fuse is that it can sometimes confuse human curiosity and contemplation with an explicit choice so be careful and test thoroughly.

Use the primary buttons for important actions.

Similar to gamepads for popular gaming systems, the controllers in VR have *primary buttons*. Save these for your most important tasks (importance = "often" and critical to the experience)

Don't Teach A New Sign Language

Humans know how to interact with the world and have various standards for doing so. Don't try to teach them an entirely new language here at the onset of VR, try to leverage natural human gestures & movements for input and interaction.

Avoid tiresome gestures.

There are certain human gestures like pulling a lever to open a door that are novel and realistic but can be fatiguing over time and aren't that meaningful. Make sure the gestures you choose are meaningful and easy to perform given the amount of times you are asking the player to perform them.

An example of a meaningful gesture would be pitching in a baseball game. Since pitching is such a fundamental part of the game and involves room for error, it makes sense to focus on designing the right gesture for pitching.

Haptic feedback controls.

Haptic feedback has been a fundamental part of video games for decades and it is becoming fundamental in virtual reality, mobile devices and more. It involves stimulating the bodily senses of the user, usually through means of vibrant pulsing. There are many haptic devices out there to enhance the virtual reality experience. Just to name a few:

- controllers, gloves (hands)
- vests, heart patches (chest)
- helmet extensions, headbands (head)
- suits (full body)

And haptic feedback can enhance controller input, movements and content interaction. Types of haptic feedback to consider when implementing with controller actions (note: not all controllers leverage haptic feedback)

1. Quick pulse – trigger proprioceptive anchors, small vibrations on hovers or selections. The tiniest of feedback tends to work just fine so don't overdo it
2. Continuous pulse – moving from A to B and the vibration grows more intense as you approach B and releases or maxes out once you reach it

You'll want to list out the inputs and parts of the experience that require haptic feedback in your strategy as you dive into the details of the prototype.

VR hot keys & gestures.

In VR, hot keys are in short supply. The remotes for VR devices have a few buttons and you should use them wisely when consider hot keys or gestures. Here are a few ideas for actions that should be considered for hot keys depending on the world you create:

*   Undo/Back Up
*   Copy/Select
*   Paste/Set
*   Delete/Destroy
*   Save/Quit
*   Switch/Insert

Teleportation control inputs.

Earlier in this book (*sorry, can't teleport you back in text =
bad joke*) I talked about using teleportation to move a user
long distances in the world. It's become quite common to
use teleportation in VR worlds because excessive movement
is fatiguing and worlds are not always small. Teleportation is
a solve for moving throughout a world without burning out
the user. Naturally, designers have come up with a variety of
ways to induce teleportation since it's important you don't
rush a user into the leap.

Point to Loft – user engages the teleportation call with their
remote and this creates a small circle on the surface of the
location they wish to move to. An arched line forms from the
user to the circle and any slight movements of the user's
remote change the position of the location. Once ready,
they release or trigger to perform the move.

Point & Pull – user engages the teleportation call and a laser
(or equivalent) points to the location they wish to travel.
When they press the trigger or let go, they are pulled (with
blur) to the new position.

Point to Room & Pull – same as Point & Pull except the user
sees a room-scale preview of the location before they
release the trigger.

Grab to Face – You can design a "teleportation object" that
transmits a user to a new location or further along in the
path. The objects can be grabbed or picked up by the user
and when pulled to their face, they will teleport.

Draw an Imperfect Circle – the user could draw a loose circle (since an accurate one is hard to draw) and once this circle drawing is enclosed, it could act as a portal to teleport somewhere else or off in the distance where they drew the circle. The size of the circle could determine the distance (but this could be dangerous if players want to toy around)

The Ride – Instead of asking the user to walk, you could design transportation mechanisms into the overall experience. Feel free to take advantage of the ones a human would already understand (train, boat, etc.) or create one from scratch.

God Mode Pick & Move – the player would engage the teleportation and it would enter them into a god view where they could pick up their player and move them about the world.

Objects that are up for grabs.

If the user is near an object and their placement of the remote means the object can be selected, you may want to indicate this "ability to select" by highlighting the object, the remote or the general area. Another trick that's been used is to fade out the remote.

Once a player selects the object, you can use haptic feedback to indicate the object has been selected. Audio, such as a ding, can have the same effect.

More on picking up objects.

Picking up objects is a common task in VR experiences that are not simply passive. Pressing an input to pick up the object and holding that input or locking it to maintain possession of the item is perhaps the most natural/intuitive action in VR controller use today. There are two primary *selection placements* for controls:

1. Direct Link – selecting the object at the remote head
2. Loose Link – selecting the object with a leading line (almost string like) so it's not stuck directly on the remote head

Some have used loose link to indicate the weight of objects you can select or to differentiate the trajectories at which objects respond to a throwing motion.

Haptic feedback can be complementary to the selection and the attachment. It acts as a *force* that's quite intuitive to the user.

The ongoing attachment of an object can be quite interactive if you build in a threshold where the object will unintendedly drop from the user's control. Here are few ideas on how to provide grip feedback when holding an object:

1. Fixed joint with haptic feedback – object attaches to the controller, repositions itself at the center or more stable part of the grip, and drops if the controller moves too fast.

2. Fixed joint with visual feedback – same as above
   except a visual meter is shown to indicate how close
   they are to dropping the object based on speed or
   grip
3. A combination of #1 and #2

Set snap points for easier object delivery.

VR users can be imprecise. Set basins for interaction
(acceptable areas around a placement task) with any task
that requires precision.

You can alleviate user frustration by embedding snap points
for certain object placements or selections so that they
accomplish the task without a perfect set.

The backpack trunk.

If the VR experience encourages the player to carry multiple
inactive items at once, it's been an intuitive and comfortable
act for people to reach over their shoulder and pull an
object into action – as if they are carrying a backpack or
something else hip and cool that houses those items.
Incorporate a backpack trunk (in any form of a pack you
wish) into your experience if you want a "real" location for
the items in the virtual world.

Naked hand inputs.

If you are designing for the future of virtual reality (possibly) or for Leap Motion Minority Report-like hand controls, then it's been shown that the most comfortable and accommodating input location is similar to where a keyboard would be for humans in the real world. While Minority Report looked badass, having inputs at eye level or higher forces the user to lift their arms which can wear on them over time. It also increases the likelihood of error because elevated arms tend to shake a bit.

Audio commands.

Audio commands are not common in VR today because there isn't a lot of support for them at the OS level yet. As audio commands become commonplace on our phones and other hardware devices and the intelligent engines that power them improve, expect more audio commands as part of the VR inputs.

Gaze inputs.

Gaze input cues rely on tracking the position of the user's gaze (headset) and objects in the world will react to a user's gaze in regards to location, timing, and more. For example, if a user looks at another character, that character may look back. There's no controller input involved, it's a simple gaze cue.

When designing these sort of cues, avoid crowding objects for a few reasons:

- If some of the gaze cues hold importance in the overall play, the user may mistake less important cues for the more critical cues located nearby
- Each cue is more impactful when you have them spaced apart. It's like being in a room with multiple people but you are only attracted to one of them. If all of them looked back at you when you shot eyes, there would be an impact, but not the one you desired. *Okay, maybe that's a bad example since that would have some sort of creepy "impact" but you get the point*
- It's simply easier to control as a designer and the player

Be careful with gaze cues because you must always remember, it's easier & more comfortable for the user to provide input with their hands/controller than it is their head.

What the hell is binmanual ambiguity?

Tilt brush is the best example of bimanual ambiguity at play. If you are not familiar with tilt brush it's an artist experience that was bought by google where the user can paint with a variety of tools.

You have two hands as the user. One paints as you move throughout the space and the other holds the pallet. When the user points the brush at the non-painting hand, it turns the experience into a 2D interaction where you pick different brushes, tools, etc. Moving your hand actually moves the space around you vs. interacting with the 3D space around it as before.

The point here being that you can change the interaction of the user's input devices when a menu, or equivalent that requires their attention, is prompted and in use.

STORYTELLING

It's story. You get it. But it is immersive, so relinquish some control.

VR is a new medium and frontier for storytelling but it doesn't change anything about the traditional elements of storytelling (characters, 3 stage arc, hero's journey, antagonist, protagonist, etc.). This means you can ideate your stories as you always have.

If you are used to telling stories in immersive and interactive environments then you'll be able to take your stories and transform them for the space. If you are not used to telling these types of immersive narratives then you should familiarize yourself with a few so that you get an idea of what it takes to pull it off. I'll give you a few insights here but the best way to start is to immersive yourself in a couple, both virtual and physical, and take notes on what worked for you vs. what didn't. When I started studying the art of immersive story, I found myself remarking and jotting notes on the following because these became the cornerstones of what made an experience good or bad:

- Am I able to string together a clear narrative based on what I just experienced?
- What was the point and what did they do to make sure it was made?
- Did I empathize with the character(s) and want to engage with them? and "why" for each main character?
- What cues did they rely on and were they clear or confusing? (sound, colors, objects, etc.)

- Any new techniques that I haven't seen before with sound, control input, cues, movement, etc. that guided or took part in the story a certain way?
- Where was I confused and why?

The audience has agency.

Freedom to look around gives the audience agency in virtual worlds and they are always active. In guiding the story though, you should use the 180 degrees is greater than 360 rule. You'll want to create a sense of direction in your story so the user feels like there is an actual narrative at play, like they don't need to look around because most of the action is happening within 180 degrees.

How do you do this? Study the age-old art form of sleight-of-hand. Audiences tend to gravitate to familiar instigators and respond to them with a sub-conscious hierarchy of elimination. For example, if they hear a bird chirp and a loud scream they are going to react to the scream before the bird and in general, will react to those cues differently.

Passive vs. active.

There are two types of story formats for VR.

1. **Passive** – the player is simply watching what's happening around them, able to look where they wish but can't actively participate with the characters or world around them. Invasion from Within is an example of this where you play one of two bunnies and simply watch the story of alien visitors unfold in front of you.

2. **Active** – the player can participate with the characters or world around them and has to take part in order for the story to progress. An example of this would be Dreadhalls, a horror game where you wander the halls of a haunted mansion and attempt to figure out why you are there, actively retrieving lighter fluid to keep your lantern lit for investigation.

The 1 thing.

There are two options when it comes to the order of story.

- Linear stories, which are most common and told in an intended order that can't be broken by the audience
- Non-linear which is somewhat open-ended and permits the audience with more control of the direction the narrative travels.

Most VR stories sit somewhere in the middle of these two because the user has agency over their view. This means you have to be methodical about getting your point across. When developing a VR story, start with the 1 thing you want your audience to walk away with. This could be a thought, empathy for other characters, new knowledge, a skill, etc. Choosing your 1 thing allows you to put some constraint around an otherwise unconstrained narrative and it's always easier to work with some north star or constraint.

VR character & POV.

After you've established your 1 thing, it's important to decide on the point-of-view you want the story told from. Here are your options

First Person
A narrative in which the main character is the player and they are viewing the story from their eyes.

First Person Peripheral
A narrative in which the player is not the main character, they are a supporting character but still see the story through their eyes.

Second Person
A narrative in which you are watching someone give instructions and they are telling the story from the perspective of "you" – it's not that common and won't be in VR so I often omit it as an option.

Third Person
A narrative in which the player is not a character and is observing while the other characters are not aware of their presence. This can be broken down into two types:

1. Third Person Limited – the observer is only able to see the story through the perspective of one characters
2. Third Person Multiple – the observer is able to follow multiple characters and has a choice. *If you choose this, ensure that there is a smooth and sensible transition as they jump between characters*

Keep it short.

Humans are still getting used to having their entire line of sight be taken up by a screen. On top of the screen, motion and head movements are taxing over time.

Early users have shared that 20 minutes is the longest amount of time they can spend in a basic and fairly stationary experience before getting fatigued to the point of taking off the headset. This limit will most definitely change as Technology gets better at putting less strain on the human eye. The best VR content falls between 5-12 minutes, and this is just a number I'm throwing out there based on my experience, various texts and the experience of my friends & family. If you are building a game that will take hours to conquer, make sure to build in natural breaking points so the user can rest their eyes.

Will VR introduce a new type of story?

I think the most impactful VR stories in the future will be considered "social experiential stories." These stories will feature multiple virtual characters that are not together in reality but are able to experience the narrative as a unit and play different roles in the story. It's not that this hasn't been done in the world of immersive storytelling or video games but VR allows it to be done from a virtual body in a virtual world. This could create all kinds of unique trails within a story and therefore make stories more than a one-hit wonder for every viewer if they enjoyed it.

One Last Thing

Room-scale VR.

For all the talk about VR UX in this book, how did it take us this long to get to the coolest part of the virtual reality promise? Room-scale VR! The ability to walk around - the Z degree of freedom!

While there are theaters that promise to bring large room scale VR to mass audiences like the movies, we are a long ways off from that audience being massive. Most of your audience will be toying with their headset in their home or apartment. This limits the actual size of the room you should design for if you are looking to reach the most people. Keep in mind that room-scale VR is only possible with high-tier devices (Oculus and Vive) and even those have recommended room size limits.

Room-scale VR is entirely dependent on the room-scale tracking setup and lucky for us, Vive and Oculus have shared their "best setup" guides to organically create a standard starting point. Room-scale VR tracking relies on motion sensing cameras. The Vive leverages 4 tracking cameras and because of this, their spec allows for the largest area which is a square of 11.5 ft. from center. Oculus recommends that you use 3 cameras which gives you a square area of 8.2 ft. from center. You can also use a 2 camera setup with Oculus which reduces the square play area to 5 ft. from center.

Besides the obvious tip to give a user grounded objects in a room-scale experience so they don't trip in confusion and hurt themselves, there isn't much material that sets room-scale experiences apart.

Because movement is typically done with a controller, you have to design your room-scale experience to account for one or the other (human walking, controller input). Don't mix the two unless there's an explicit break in the experience when alternating between them.

If you learned nothing from this book, at least take these core principles with you:

1. Optimize for performance
2. Prioritize Comfort
3. Prioritize Ease of Learning
4. Avoid Being Too Literal
5. Sound is Critical
6. Don't Break Presence

THE END FOR NOW

For updates on VR UX – **follow Casey Fictum on medium.com**

Thank you so much for taking the time to read VR UX – I am humbled and appreciative of the support.

Please leave a review on Amazon – all feedback is welcome & 5 stars are kind to my loan debt!

Feel free to reach out on Linkedin if you want to chat VR or simply become friends.

54211052R00071

Made in the USA
San Bernardino, CA
10 October 2017